THE 2 MINUTE
TESTER

33 Routines to Make You a Better QAT Professional

DAVID BRUCE

Copyright © 2021
DAVID BRUCE
MJJP Consulting Ltd.
THE 2 MINUTE TESTER
33 Routines to Make You a Better QAT Professional
All rights reserved.

No part of this publication may be reproduced, distributed, or transmitted in any form or by any means, including photocopying, recording, or other electronic or mechanical methods, without the prior written permission of the publisher, except in the case of brief quotations embodied in critical reviews and certain other non-commercial uses permitted by copyright law.

DAVID BRUCE
MJJP Consulting Ltd.

Printed in the United Kingdom
First Printing 2021
First Edition 2021

10 9 8 7 6 5 4 3 2 1

Limit of Liability/Disclaimer of Warranty
All information given in this book, Two-Minute Tester, is based upon individual research and experience of the author. David Bruce cannot be held responsible for the consequences of actions taken as a result of using the information contained in this book. All information is used at your own risk. While all information is checked for accuracy, no liability can be inferred from use of same.

Two-Minute Tester
Is a trademark of David Bruce and is used under licence.

Dedication

For Catherine, James and Millie,

All my love.

TABLE OF CONTENTS

WHO THIS BOOK IS FOR? 1

ABOUT THE AUTHOR 4

1 EXPLORATORY TESTING 5

2 EFFECTIVE TEAM WORKING IN QAT 7

3 THE TESTER MINDSET: 80/20 9

4 RISK-BASED TESTING: TEST TECHNIQUES 11

5 STATIC TESTING: TEST TECHNIQUES 14

6 BUILDING YOUR OWN AVENGERS TEAM I: RECRUITMENT 17

7 SPECIFICATION BY EXAMPLE, OR TRUE LIVING DOCUMENTATION: TEST TECHNIQUES 20

8 USER ACCEPTANCE TESTING (UAT): TEST TECHNIQUES 23

9 TEST TEAM LEADERSHIP: MANAGEMENT 25

10 DEALING WITH MANAGEMENT OR 'WAIT, WHAT DO YOU GUYS DO AGAIN?' 27

11 SWOT AND HOW IT CAN HELP YOUR QA DELIVERY: TEST TECHNIQUES 29

12 BECOMING A TEST MANAGER (I): MANAGEMENT 32

13 BECOMING A TEST MANAGER (II): MANAGEMENT 34

14 GDPR: DATA 36

15 RUNNING A DEFECT BOARD/TRIAGE MEETING 38

16 MACHINE LEARNING IN TESTING: THE CYBORGS ARE COMING… TRENDS 40

17 SOFT SKILLS 43

18 WRITING A GREAT BUG REPORT: TEST TECHNIQUES 45

19 PROCESSES TO IMPROVE QA PROCESSES 47

20 JOINING IT UP AND LOOKING FOR THE BREAKS: INTEGRATION ..50

21 COMPANY CULTURE: OR AVOIDING REJECTION 52

22 MANAGEMENT: PROBLEM-SOLVING IN QA MANAGEMENT – THE THREE PS IN QA 54

23 CONTINUOUS IMPROVEMENT (KAIZEN) 56

24 RISK MITIGATION: STOP IT GOING WRONG BEFORE IT DOES..58

25 DEFECTS ADDING TO THE PRODUCT BACKLOG AND THE RISK TO YOUR PROJECT 60

26 KEEPING IT ALL ON TRACK: DAILY, WEEKLY AND MONTHLY TASKS 62

27 TRACKING QA PROJECT PROGRESS (WATERFALL) 67

28 STAND-UPS: THE POWER OF INTROVERTS 70

29 EFFECTIVE COMMUNICATION 73

30 FINANCE: BUDGETS AND QA 75

31 PRODUCTIVITY: THE POWER OF NEXT ACTION STEPS – KEEPING MOMENTUM 78

32 MANAGEMENT: DELEGATION 81

33 MANAGEMENT: THE FEEDBACK LOOP 3 TO 1 RULE 83

APPENDIX A 86

WHO THIS BOOK IS FOR?

Let's get one thing clear, I **can't** make you a tester in two minutes. What **I can** do is break testing tips and tricks into chunks that can be read and absorbed in two minutes. These tips cover most areas of testing and are based on best practice and learning the hard way.

When I started within QAT there were numerous resources about what you should know as a tester but none about **becoming** a tester. Long articles, books and online resources explained what black box testing was, how risk-based testing was supposed to work.

What they **didn't** explain was how to communicate the results of your testing, how to build a test team or how to get the most out of your more reticent test team members.

What this book does is blend the soft skills with the hard skills, because each one taken in isolation **won't** make you a better tester.

You can be the most amazing technical tester but if you can't communicate your findings, your ability to progress is limited. Similarly, if you can speak for hours on any subject but you don't have the background ability to back this up then you are lost as a tester.

Blending the soft skills with the hard skills will make you a better tester. Over 25 years of testing I have learned the lessons, some easy, some much harder, that make a tester successful in their field and how they can make a real difference. A note on wording. I use the word **tester** throughout this book; however, this term is meant to cover every level of tester. Unless specifically focused on test management then test manager will be used.

In addition, QAT, quality assurance and testing, where assurance is key, is implied here. So, if you work solely in QA then this book is meant for you too. Assurance requires a deep understanding of testing techniques as well as specific assurance skills, which will be covered here.

This book is aimed at professionals who could be just starting their journey in QAT, are midpoint in their career or are operating at senior level. The aim of this book is that you, as the reader, can dip in and out of specific sections to get advice and tips for areas you may already be familiar with or on areas you aren't so clear about.

HOW TO USE THIS BOOK

You can simply read the book, section by section. Each section is designed to be readable within two minutes and give you an easily digestible element to work with, do further investigation or simply increase your understanding.

PROBLEM-SOLVING

If you have a specific problem that needs resolution, the different sections of this book are broken down into the following themes: bear in mind that one section may well cover multiple themes.

- Test management
- Test assurance
- Test recruitment
- Agile testing
- Waterfall testing
- Non-functional testing
- Data
- Tools
- Test accelerators
- Automation
- Testing trends
- Test techniques
- Problem-solving
- Leadership

ABOUT THE AUTHOR

David Bruce has worked in software testing and assurance for over 25 years. In that time, he has worked in QA practices in both the public sector and in the private sector in the UK, Ireland and Australia. He has run large QA practices with up to 24 separate projects and worked for start-ups with one or two projects. As an MBA graduate, he is always interested in the nexus between QA and programme management, looking at the commonalities between them and how best practices can be delivered.

He is passionate about cutting through the jargon to deliver high-quality QA services and aims with this book to share these lessons learned and best practices, whether you are starting on your career in QA or are further down the track in terms of QA management or programme management.

1 EXPLORATORY TESTING

You don't have much time.

You don't know the system.

They need it tested.

Exploratory testing is a useful technique when there isn't much time available, you need the system tested quickly and you know little or nothing about the system under test.

The concept is to move **fast** and identify the weaknesses in the system.

Documentation is kept to a minimum, normally test collateral is limited to the outputs from testing (i.e. defects found). In some cases, for audit purposes, there may be a need to describe the exploratory approach.

Some approaches are:

1) **Timeboxed:** as time is usually a constraining factor, this is a frequent approach, for example, a 45-minute run.

2) **Paired testing**: this technique is useful, two testers work through the system under test and work as a team to test the system.

3) **Pre-investigation**: talking with devs and BAs to get an overview of the system, where the integration points and where the most complex areas are of the entire system. This is often a useful technique, especially where underlying documentation is either sparse or non-existent.

You can execute exploratory testing at any time in the SDLC. It is often most effective either at the beginning or end of a specific test phase, for example, the start of UAT, or if operating in an agile manner, at the end of each sprint, once automated and other specific functional tests have been executed.

KEY TAKEAWAYS

√ Keep it short in terms of time.

√ Leave your documentation to the end, make notes as you go when you find defects.

√ Focus on integration points.

2 EFFECTIVE TEAM WORKING IN QAT

'**Invert, always invert.**' – **Charlie Munger**

What makes an effective QAT team? Often it makes sense to invert the question. What makes an ineffective QAT team? If you have experience of more than a few years working in QAT, you will have seen or worked in, ineffective or worse teams. These normally share certain characteristics:

a) Siloed thinking: 'Well, the bit I tested is fine, not my problem if there is an issue somewhere else.'

b) Sole fount of wisdom: 'Bob is the only guy who knows how and what these tests actually do.'

c) We are at war with everyone!: 'The devs hate us, the BAs hate us, hell, even the PM hates us!'

Doubtless you can think of more examples. The aim here is to look at what causes such problems and prevent them from occurring.

Tactics for avoiding them can be seen in the following:

1) **Start with the whole solution in mind**. While you may be testing one specific area of the system, how does it logically flow into the wider picture? For example, with 10 specific GUI screens under test, you may be responsible for 5, can you build a whole of system smoke test to exercise all 10, even though they are not specifically under your remit?

2) **Share the knowledge**. Paired testing, paired automated test creation, regular QAT specific show and tells, and central knowledge repositories all make this more effective.

3) **Collaborate**. This will be developed more in Section 20; however, stop thinking of devs as people whose work you are trying to find fault with and start with the view that you are helping them deliver the very best solution possible. Tactics such as 3 Amigos sessions are incredibly helpful before each sprint in agile, while in waterfall you have to have regular check-in sessions with devs prior to testing their work.

KEY TAKEAWAYS

√ Invert: ask how would I make this team ineffective and do the opposite.

√ Think whole system, what is the system attempting to do?

√ Share the knowledge!

√ Collaborate.

3 THE TESTER MINDSET: 80/20

You make it, we break it.

A tester has to focus on the customer need. Your developers and BAs also share this view but come about in a very different way. Devs want to build cool stuff that blows the customer away. BAs want to come up with new and shiny ways to excite the customer.

You want to make sure that all this stuff works. And you want to know what happens when you don't follow the path you expect the customer to follow but rather go off on a tangent.

Pareto

Pareto was an Italian economist and engineer who coined the 80/20 rule. He observed that 80% of results came from 20% of causes. Too often testers focus on their testing from an 80% happy path approach and 20% negative. This focuses testing in the wrong direction. It should be reversed.

Your testing should focus 80% of your efforts on the unhappy path. What if the user does **not** follow the standard route in your application?

What if they go nuts and keep backtracking? What if they click the **Submit** button twenty times?

Can the system respond or do they get random timeouts or other errors?

Ideally your happy paths are automated and are executed swiftly. This gives you confidence that your baseline is solid. Then you can focus on the (often more interesting) side of looking at ways the system can fail. This is not restricted to paths, but also to garbage data. Data negative testing also lends itself to automation. Regardless of how you execute it, you need to hit it hard.

As your suite of tests increase (if you are testing in an iterative, agile manner), more and more of your negative tests should be automated, with only the edge, complex to test cases remaining for manual testing.

KEY TAKEAWAYS

✓ Focus on the 80/20.

✓ Automate your happy path.

✓ Don't forget your data testing.

4 RISK-BASED TESTING: TEST TECHNIQUES

'Risk comes from not knowing what you're doing.'

– Warren Buffett

Risk-based testing is a popular approach when you don't have much time to test and you need to test the most important, or riskiest, parts of the solution. How do you define risky though? The focus is on **key functionality** of the system, the **likelihood** that they will fail and the **impact** of failure. Once you understand these three variables you can plan accordingly.

Key Functionality ⊠ Likelihood of failure ⊠ Impact of failure.

Gaining information on these three variables can come from your own system knowledge or through discussion with subject matter experts, the key focus is on how you can get clarity quickly on likely failure points. This then leads to the prioritisation of specific test scenarios over others. But how can you prioritise specific test cases over others?

Look at it from a new versus legacy view, complex versus simple – are there multiple, complex paths or single path options? What changes have been made if a legacy system? If a new system, what are the most complex elements? Then, look at **connectivity** and **integration** points.

Specifically, does the functionality integrate with multiple endpoints, has the functionality been tested previously end to end at any point? Or have only stubs or emulators been used? If that is the case, those areas need to be top of your risk-based list for testing first.

Then you have the **likelihood of failure**. This is based on how extensively the system has been tested, what is the experience level of the development team and how integrated is it with the rest of the solution. This will be a more nuanced judgement call on your part. This can be more challenging if you are new to the project as opposed to an embedded tester. If you are new then there is value in discussing with your BA, development lead and technical design lead (if there is one) to get a clearer view on possible failure points.

Impact of failure as your last element centres around the question, if this part of the solution fails is the ship dead in the water? Or, if this piece fails can users navigate around it, largely unimpacted? Examples of this are a payment function within an online store. If the system cannot process payments it doesn't matter how brilliant and smooth an experience the user has had up until then.

Conversely, again, with the online store analogy, if a user cannot mark their purchase as a gift and hence have it treated in a different way by the system – for example, hiding the price of the product – then, while annoying, it does not kill the user experience.

KEY TAKEAWAYS

✓ Focus on key functionality, less so on edge cases.

✓ What is likelihood of failure? Integration points a good place to start.

✓ What is impact of failure? A failed payment step will render worthless all preceding elements to the customer.

5 STATIC TESTING: TEST TECHNIQUES

Static testing is the testing of a product without executing actual tests against the product.

It involves examination of the specifications from a QA perspective and challenging how testable they are. Its great benefit is that it is done very **early** in the development cycle, enabling remedies to be made cheaply.

In terms of tools it is hard to beat the human eye for static testing. However, using the basic search function in Word or Excel gives you a method for consistently checking for the occurrence of specific words. You can search for ambiguous words such as **should, may, could, possibly, approximately** and so on and highlight where they occur. This is a useful first step, especially for longer requirements documents. There are macros available that let you search for multiple words at once, very useful for longer requirements documents.

Running searches such as this also provides useful metrics to the specification providers – the BAs, architects, systems designers – in terms of ambiguity. If you can say there are 23 ambiguous elements within a design and this is what they are you will get a lot more buy-in than saying, '**Well, it's a bit ambiguous in parts**'.

Specifications are not the only area that can be static tested. Almost all collateral can be static tested, for example:

- Prototype designs
- System, unit, performance tests
- Code review
- Business flow documents (goes by a variety of names, often called user journeys too)
- Architectural diagrams

A subset within static testing is technical validation. This focuses on the coding protocols, for example, user input validation, handling of incorrect data and user journeys where end users can travel in non-linear fashion (e.g. they start on one screen, move forward three steps, then change their mind and want to change data in the first screen).

Static testing tools that can be used for technical validation are many and varied. Generally, these run against existing source code and produce a report highlighting weaknesses in coding practices that developers can use to remedy their code. In practice, with modern IDE (integrated development environments), an awful lot of code quality testing is done as the developer codes.

However, standalone static tools are especially good at highlighting gaps in security from a coding perspective and contribute greatly to overall system quality. Some tools to think about are SourceMeter (and the basic version is free) and CheckStyle (open source but only works against Java code).

KEY TAKEAWAYS

✓ Call out ambiguity where it appears in documentation, the earlier you catch it the better.

✓ Statistics are best when describing how ambiguous documents are.

✓ Static testing tools include SourceMeter and Checkstyle.

6 BUILDING YOUR OWN AVENGERS TEAM I: RECRUITMENT

Let's face it, the Avengers would be pretty dull if they were all just Hulks, Iron Men or Thors. What gives them their strength as a team is their diversity and it's hard to think of a more diverse team than Black Widow, Thanos and Thor, for example.

Almost all high-performing QA teams have an element of diversity, be it background, experience or skills. Even what we would consider relatively homogenous high-performing teams, such as football or rugby, have differences in approach and mindset. What they do share is a focus on what good looks like, what the end result is and where they see how they can contribute individually to this.

How do you make this happen? You hire for difference from yourself. Look around the table at your current team. If they look like you, then you don't have a diverse team. You have a set of skills, what you should be looking at is hiring those with skills that are different from you. Naturally there is a base level of competency you expect, after that, however, you need to look at differences to your mindset, ways of working, skills and experience to yours to leverage the most that you can from a diverse team.

I managed a team where we had people from 27 different countries, each with their own experiences and expertise. They were fantastically talented, and crucially, we had many valid and different viewpoints on addressing issues that arose from a delivery or technical perspective that helped us deliver some great products. I firmly believe that if we had a homogenous, all-male or all-female team we would not have been as creative, effective or productive.

Bear in mind that a more diverse team means that decision-making can be less collaborative and more confrontational. As you have so many different viewpoints there is always the risk that it will be harder to get to a high-quality decision. However, that is the point, the more diversity you have the higher quality overall decision-making will be. It's not comfortable all the time but it is highly effective.

Just to be clear, however, you cannot discriminate in any way in your hiring process, although you can choose to hire for difference. I dress pretty formally when I am in a work situation, and one day, I interviewed an automation engineer for a role. He arrived in a flowery Hawaiian shirt, wore shorts and sandals. He looked like he was headed to the beach. I'm not sure he would have got past the front door in most consultancies. What followed was one of the most interesting interviews I've ever had. He had a fantastic background of working in start-ups as well as in large corporates. He was engaging and passionate about what he did. He turned out to be one of my best hiring decisions, his team loved him, he built an outstanding automation framework and was generally a great person to have on the team.

Build your own Avengers team!

KEY TAKEAWAYS

✓ Base competence is critical but after that you are looking at divergent experiences and mindsets.

✓ If everyone in the team has the same background, gender and experiences you don't have a diverse team.

✓ For more on this read the excellent whitepaper on diversity in teams from **Harvard Business Review** entitled '**Diverse teams feel less comfortable and that's why they perform better**'. hbr.org/2016/09

7 SPECIFICATION BY EXAMPLE, OR TRUE LIVING DOCUMENTATION: TEST TECHNIQUES

Specification by example is a mode of developing and releasing software that was first conceptualised by Gojko Adjic in his excellent book of the same name. His concept addresses some of the main problems that we see over and over in software engineering. Namely the disconnect between what is specified and what is built and how to keep track of changes that are made throughout an engineering project.

Gojko's brilliant concept is to make the requirements the delivery, make them readable to anyone, BAs, QAs, developers, project managers, technical and non-technical members of the team. As a result, you then have a clear, understandable, set of statements in **given**, **when**, **then f**ormat. The essence of it is to reduce abstraction and ambiguity and replace with **specific** and **realistic** examples.

The heart of it is using concrete examples, reducing abstraction. If you do this the chances of misinterpretation are reduced, developers love it as they aren't dealing with ambiguity and QA love it as they have a very clear set of requirements to work against. Very often you will hear people talk about '**One source of truth**' when they refer to specification by example (SBE) and that is not a bad way of describing it. Another way is calling it **living documentation**.

What you will find is that your devs and BAs love it almost as much as the QA team, as they all can understand what is being delivered.

To make specification by example possible requires Cucumber; this BDD (behaviour-driven development) language has the power of simplicity and clarity, look at the example below:

Specification By Example: Joe's Gardening Goods

Feature: product must have value added tax (VAT) added at 20% to purchase price.

- UK customers pay VAT.
- Non-UK customers don't pay VAT.
- VAT is applied at checkout payment screen.
- VAT is calculated by shipping address.

Given: the product has been selected by the customer.

When: the customer pays for the product

Then: the customer is charged the correct rate of VAT.

It should be made clear that this is not only a change in QA practices but also in dev and BA practices. It is an incredibly powerful way of reducing ambiguity and not only building things right but also building the right things. One caveat to introducing specification by example is that it can take time to implement. Where I have been involved in implementing this you need to be aware that is as much a cultural as a technical change to ways of working.

KEY TAKEAWAYS

✓ Read Gojko's excellent book for some in-depth insights into how you can implement specification by example.

✓ Remember it isn't just QA, it covers development, business analysis and project management as well.

✓ SBE is not something that can be done overnight, it requires changes in processes and tooling, but the payoffs are big.

8 USER ACCEPTANCE TESTING (UAT): TEST TECHNIQUES

You have almost reached your goal for release of your product, the final hurdle is user acceptance testing. It's worthwhile to remember the definition of UAT: one that I like is **real** users using the **real** system to run through **real** business processes.

Often the argument is why do you need UAT once you have run through all your previous phases of testing? The key part of the puzzle, however – the end users – is usually missing from those earlier phases. The key requirements may have been tested but the nuances as to how the software is actually used could well be missed.

To create UAT test cases there is a need to work very closely with business analysts and end users of the system (if an internal-facing system). If you have an external-facing system you can still conduct UAT, ideally with members of the public who will end up as the users, but your test case creation will be more driven by your product owner.

Your role as a QAT professional during UAT should be to act as an **enabler**. You are enabling the business users to access the system under test, provide guidance where necessary and act as the collator of all the defects, observations and enhancements.

You should look at all roles that can use your system and plan accordingly. A good rule of thumb is to start with most restricted user rights: UAT should confirm that users can't access areas they don't have rights to, all the way through to the admin role that should be able to do everything. So, go with most locked down to least locked down.

Have a defect review board call at close of testing every day. Review all issues encountered and log as:

- **Defects**: it doesn't work the way it should.
- **Observations**: it's a bit unusual, the user journey goes this way but it doesn't stop the user completing the action.
- **Enhancements**: it takes 5 clicks to reach this point, it could easily be done in 3 if the design was tweaked slightly.

All of the above applies to a waterfall delivery approach. However, in an agile delivery team, a different approach is needed. Options include having a UAT specific environment as one of your test environments. Then, using this at specific points in sprints, for example, having end users scheduled in at the same time in every sprint, to exercise end-user journeys. As the definition of **done in a sprint** is that you have a shippable, complete piece of functionality, this is one way of making sure that UAT is covered correctly.

KEY TAKEAWAYS

√ Be very clear how you categorise any issues you find, for example, defects, observations, enhancements.

√ Act as an enabler/facilitator.

√ Cover all user roles.

9 TEST TEAM LEADERSHIP: MANAGEMENT

Test team leadership is all about the drive to empower and direct individual team members to deliver what is needed by the project or programme. Gone are the days when you set out your grand vision, wander off and berate the team when they haven't delivered what you told them to.

As mentioned in Section 6, your team is hopefully composed of individuals with different experiences and backgrounds. Your role is to describe what good looks like, for example, 'Defect-free release of system A in 8 weeks with 35 specific user flows fully functional and able to cope with 10,000 concurrent users'.

If you are working in an agile manner, then you will be working closely with your product owner and lead developer to place these requirements in a more granular context and add them to the backlog to be worked on.

Your team will of course be involved with this process through stand-ups and sprint planning and then will look at the mechanisms for how they plan on testing through the delivery cycle. This could be in terms of how the continuous delivery pipeline will either be configured to cope with the expected changes or set up from scratch.

Your role is to coach, be a sounding board for ideas about how to test and above all remove blockers that your team may encounter.

If you are in a waterfall delivery team then there will equally be scope for QA team members to exercise creative approaches to QA of what is delivered by the dev team. Again, your role is to set the outlines, be there to bounce ideas off and remove blockers.

In both agile and waterfall you need to resist the urge to micromanage as this lessens chances for your team to learn. An alternative can be to suggest options when a particular approach isn't working due to time, for example, '**You have an awful lot of negative tests, have you looked at commonality among them so we can safely reduce the number yet maintain coverage?**'

When pushed in terms of answers, a simple but effective approach is to ask the team, 'What do you think should be done?' The team will very likely already know what they should do, your role is to provide and build their confidence that they are going in the right direction. Of course, if they are wildly off tangent, your duty is to tell them this too and steer them back on to the correct path.

KEY TAKEAWAYS

✓ Resist the urge to micromanage.

✓ Ask questions; don't offer what you think the answer is immediately.

✓ Set the strategy, let the team focus on the tactical.

✓ Coach for both positive and negative behaviours.

✓ Reduce blockers, you should be the enabler.

10 DEALING WITH MANAGEMENT OR 'WAIT, WHAT DO YOU GUYS DO AGAIN?'

A perennial issue when dealing with senior management is that they don't get what you do in QAT. This is still an issue with less technically adept managers and can cause problems, such as shortening development or release lifecycles without understanding the risk to a quality delivery. Reasons why senior managers don't understand QA or its importance can usually be put down to a lack of exposure to what exactly QA professionals do.

This is a problem you need to own and resolve. Specifically, you need to brief them on how QA is not about breaking things but rather acts as an enabler to higher quality delivery, and through technologies (such as Jmeter) and ways of working (such as specification by example), a well-functioning QA team can shorten delivery timelines while maintaining high quality.

Some ways in which you can share this information with senior management:

- Bring them to quick (10-minute) show-and-tell sessions showing a specific tool in action, for example, Selenium Grid, Jmeter or Browserstack.
- Attend 3 Amigos session within agile delivery team, these always give a really good insight into how central QA, BA and devs work together to deliver great products.

- Get them to a weekly stand-up: if you manage more than one QA team, a weekly stand-up across the teams to discuss upcoming plans and blockers is a great way for senior management to understand QA.
- In a waterfall project, demonstrate how QA works to drive out ambiguities in the requirements either through static testing or, even better, by running the requirements through a simple macro called ABC (ambiguity checking) that looks for ambiguous words such as **may, might, could** and **should**, flags them up and displays them for resolution by the BA.
- Where you have a dashboard (for example, in a continuous integration delivery), then step them through the different elements of the dashboard, emphasising the cycling of software through different environments and automated tests running before promotion to live.

KEY TAKEAWAYS

√ Where you can, demonstrate, and not with PowerPoint. Show them the testing tools in action.

√ Emphasise faster, better quality delivery. It's no longer '**You make it, we break it**'. It is now '**We collaborate to make it**'.

√ QAT done correctly should add value and reduce risks greatly.

11 SWOT AND HOW IT CAN HELP YOUR QA DELIVERY: TEST TECHNIQUES

A favoured tool in management consultancies is the SWOT exercise. This is a two by two square, showing strengths, weaknesses, opportunities and threats. How does this help in QAT?

Two ways: firstly, at the beginning of your QA project, it focuses efforts on areas that need attention.

Secondly, if you are brought into a troubled project and need to rapidly get up to speed with the underlying issues, it helps to bring these to the surface very quickly. You should aim to have 3 points in each of the areas.

For example, this is a SWOT diagram for an existing project that has been running a while but has clear issues.

SWOT example for QA team

Strengths	Weaknesses
■ Highly experienced QA team ■ Regression already partially automated ■ BA/QA relationship good.	■ QA/dev relationship poor ■ Requirements very unclear ■ Delivery is always late

Opportunities	Threats
■ Non-functional testing can be integrated within existing testing frameworks already in use ■ QAT team-wide sharing of best practice in tooling and processes a great opportunity ■ Automation can be accelerated	■ Real risk of budget cuts ■ QA team at risk of losing contract to rival consultancy ■ Scope creep

To do a proper SWOT analysis you need to talk not only to the QA team but also to dev, BA, PMs and anyone else you think may have valid observations. Once you pull the strands together, you need to look at how to address the weaknesses in a structured manner. Are there processes you can put in place, for example, weekly or daily stand-ups; are there tools you can use, such as ABC (ambiguity counter); or are there more fundamental changes you need to make, such as personnel?

Use the SWOT as your map to next actions, focus on the weaknesses, but don't neglect the opportunities; in the example above, could performance tests be built into the current automation framework?

KEY TAKEAWAYS

√ Talk to as many people as possible to get a proper picture.

√ Be as specific as you can, avoid ambiguity.

√ Strengths and weaknesses are usually internal to the project.

√ Opportunities and threats are usually but not always external to the project: however, within QAT, you can interpret this loosely, for example, the matrix above shows 3 opportunities available to the project internally.

- For an excellent, more comprehensive explanation of SWOT, I recommend the Harvard Business Review piece on SWOT here:
- http://119.226.62.30:8081/gurukul/02_HBR_Tools_SWOT_Guide.pdf

12 BECOMING A TEST MANAGER (I): MANAGEMENT

This was my first gig as a test manager and everyone was annoyed with me. The BAs, devs, hell, even the project manager was seriously annoyed. I was seen as the blocker, the killjoy, couldn't I just get with the plan? The problem was that the company wanted to release software and I was stopping them, as I said too many items on the exit gate were red.

I was overruled by senior management and they went ahead and released the software anyway. Sure enough, it was buggy as hell and got pulled. Now our customers were pissed. I didn't feel any better being vindicated, everyone still hated me.

What could I have done differently? This was a waterfall project so inevitably there were elements that I didn't get access to until the final mile. However, there were things I could and should have done.

- **I didn't set expectations**: they didn't know what I needed for all elements on the gate to go green.
- **I didn't communicate**: the first time they showed up I told them we weren't going to go for release. Nobody, and I mean nobody, likes surprises like this.
- **I didn't see it from their point of view**: as a developer you develop, you build. No one likes being told that something they built isn't any good.

A quick reference then is **communicate, set** and **see**. Breaking this down further means getting involved as early in the process as possible, if you don't have this luxury then you are going to have to move fast to close the gaps, let the team know what is expected of them but in a collaborative and diplomatic manner. An all guns blazing approach, demanding as opposed to persuading is guaranteed to backfire.

Set means that once you have communicated what you need then you set up the processes for reviews on progress and where the project stands with blockers.

See is the final element, your final review and agreement to release.

KEY TAKEAWAYS

✓ Lose the ego, it's not all about you.

✓ Communicate, set and see.

✓ Set clear expectations, if you do **X** I will do **Y**, happy days.

✓ Communicate: let them know ahead of time what you need to go green, don't spring it on them.

✓ Empathise: instead of telling them '**This is not going to work**', focus on the positive, such as '**You guys have done some amazing stuff, what I just need is for you to clear the following**'. Once you look at the world from the dev and BA perspective, things get a lot clearer and your job as a QA professional is much more straightforward. Empathise, don't tell.

13 BECOMING A TEST MANAGER (II): MANAGEMENT

So you've gotten a few years of testing under your belt, you want to get ahead, what do you do?

Show that you can own problems: own a difficult piece of work no one else is interested in. Then look at solving the issues.

Show that you can lead a team: this can be difficult if you are the only QA on the team. A solution can well be to look at leading the wider team. There may well be a PM but there is nothing to stop you approaching her or him and asking if you could support some of the wider project delivery elements. These may not be directly QA related but will give you exposure to project delivery.

Learn about leading: two ways. One, get a mentor, or two, do a lot of reading in this space. I have actually done both; each has its own advantages but it's the goal in mind, not the way you get there.

If you are part of a large organisation, ask to spend some time with the lead QA individual on the team and potentially shadow them. Ask lots of questions.

Reading in this space: there are some good books in this area focused specifically on QA and the enormous topic of management has endless excellent books and other resources that can help you.

One great resource is the book **The Four-Hour Workweek**. Despite the title this isn't about doing all your work in four hours! Rather, the author, Tim Ferriss, really helps you to differentiate between being busy and being effective and ruthlessly eliminating the busy things that aren't moving you forward.

Checking your email 20 times a day anyone?

Another excellent book is **High Output Management** by Andy Grove of Intel. This gives some great insights into leading technical organisations and he explains in a very clear and concise manner ways to improve how you manage and lead.

Understanding your organisation: each organisation has its own culture, processes and hierarchy. Part of becoming an effective QA manager is understanding how the QA function is viewed and operates within your organisation.

With this understanding comes clarity about how you should communicate and operate as a manager. Where QA is treated as a trusted source of information, your management style upwards should be more direct, where QA is less trusted, you need to be more subtle in your delivery.

KEY TAKEAWAYS

√ Own a gnarly problem.

√ Lead a team or show leadership within a team.

√ Learn as much as you can about leadership and the latest practices (see Sections 9 and y for more information on this).

√ Learn by doing.

14 GDPR: DATA

GDPR is legislation enacted since 2018 covering the protection of any personal data that could be used to identify an EU citizen. Penalties are high for non-compliance, ranging up to 4% of global revenue or 20 million euros, whichever is greater. What this means for QAT is that the way in which you manage and control your data if you operate within the EU, or you operate elsewhere in the world but your data is stored within the EU, needs to include clear protocols to follow.

These are your data policies, specifically:

- None of your data that you use for testing purposes should be traceable back to an individual, in effect you should not be able to identify a person from this data.
- This does not just mean the obvious data points such as date of birth, addresses and name. It can also include other ways in which users can be identified such as general location data, cookies, IP addresses and even things such as devices.
- If you haven't already done so, you should conduct a data audit to confirm what data you already have for QA purposes and confirm nothing is identifiable to a specific individual.
- Check whether there is a data protection officer appointed to your group or wider company. If there is one, consult with them on what processes of templates you should be using to ensure compliance.

- Test data management is your biggest area of focus for GDPR compliance. Where in the past we would have used a copy of production data to execute testing, to do so now would be in breach of GDPR. The focus should be on anonymisation of this data from production before it is used in any form of testing.
- When it comes to anonymisation of data there are circumstances where even if pseudonyms are used, they could still be in breach of GDPR as it may be possible to still identify an individual from their pseudonym.
- One of the more effective ways of dealing with the data challenge is to use synthetic data. This removes the risk of actual user data ever being exposed and thus your risk profile is greatly reduced. There may be edge cases where you will need to use actual data but in the vast majority of cases, synthetic data should meet your needs.
- There are a large number of synthetic data creation tools available, they vary in price and the clear determinant is usually the database that is supported.
- Your discovery work should focus on what you have already; bear in mind that it is very often infrequently used datasets that are most likely to be a source of non-compliant data.

KEY TAKEAWAYS

√ Do a data audit.

√ Find out who your data protection manager is.

√ Use synthetic data if possible.

15 RUNNING A DEFECT BOARD/TRIAGE MEETING

Defect review boards (DRBs) sometimes known as defect triage meetings, are used in both agile and waterfall projects and programmes. They are a process for reviewing in a systematic manner open defects and assessing their severity, impact and version in which they will be fixed. They are also a forum for development to challenge whether they are indeed a defect at all or are an enhancement or general observation. Generally, they are held 2 or 3 times a week but can flex depending on the project.

DRBs within a waterfall project are dictated by the test phases and the test schedule. For example, during a phase of UAT (1-week phase) a number of defects are found by QAT and subject matter experts. Your defect review board should be thinking about putting those defects into three buckets:

- Fix now
- Fix later
- Fix never (i.e. it's not a defect)

People who should be in your DRB include at a minimum your project manager, dev manager (or senior developer) and test manager (or senior tester). If you have a larger project then you could also include a product manager and business analyst. However, bear in mind, the more people you have on your board, the longer it will take to get through these defects.

Rules for running an effective defect board:

KEY TAKEAWAYS

✓ Keep notes: I've lost count of defect boards where no one can remember the actions required. If possible, update defects as you go in your defect management tool.

✓ Have an agenda and stick to it: if you have 20 defects to review make sure you review all 20.

✓ Stick to time: timebox the DRB. The danger is that dev and QA get stuck in very long convoluted discussions. If you have a complicated defect that requires very in-depth analysis, then park it and move on. Agree to have a separate discussion to review.

✓ Stick to time II: don't have your DRB over 4 hours long, keep it tight and short!

✓ Own them: make sure defects are assigned, either to the dev team or even better to an individual.

✓ Clarity: have a QA pre-board review. This simply confirms that all defects that are to be reviewed have the following:

- a clear description (no ambiguity! No mays, coulds, mights in there)
- a severity assigned
- a priority assigned
- a status assigned
- the person who raised it detailed

16 MACHINE LEARNING IN TESTING: THE CYBORGS ARE COMING... TRENDS

Machine learning, one of the buzzwords in testing at the moment, is still at a relatively nascent stage in the QAT space with a number of small companies pushing the boundaries of what is possible. Broadly, machine learning can be used for:

- Test script creation
- Test script execution
- Test data creation

There are a number of commercial tools that can assist in this process and their focus is very much on pattern recognition. Two of the more interesting tools are Appvance and Functionize. They are both commercial tools. As at time of writing, there are no open-source AI/machine learning tools available but keep checking, it is only a matter of time before this changes.

In a nutshell, Appvance has what it calls level-5 autonomy; there are certainly echoes of automation within the car industry, where their machine learning algorithm generates regression tests automatically with claimed 100% test coverage.

This is focused on Web applications and mobile apps at the moment and shows promise, but early days yet; as more functionality is released this should be a tool to watch. Appvance currently covers the functional, performance and security tiers.

As always in QA, your aim is a balance of what is achievable with tooling and you need to bear in mind what data you are willing to share with your test tool provider. If you work in a highly secure environment, you need to consider what data, if any, your security team will allow to be shared with a third-party tool provider. With machine learning the use of training datasets needs to be considered and how this can be accessed. If not, what forms of anonymised data are going to be of use in building automated test creation and execution?

Functionize take a different tack, you can interact with the system under test and the machine learning algorithms will track your interactions and extend these into a complete test suite. Or, you can write your tests in plain English (shades of specification by example, see Section 7) and the system will translate these into complete test cases using what they call their NLP technologies.

It is early days in AI-driven automation testing but systems such as those above show promise and they are something to look at, especially where you may have a user intensive GUI under test and the workload of creating and maintaining tests is growing massively. Also, tools such as Appvance and Functionize can help with mobile app testing.

KEY TAKEAWAYS

✓ Have a look at https://www.appvance.ai/

✓ And also https://www.functionize.com

✓ Check about data policies and whether data can be shared with vendors, especially as will be cloud hosted.

17 SOFT SKILLS

You can be the best tester in the world but if you can't communicate in a clear and effective manner, you are not going to progress in the world. Similarly, you can be incredibly brilliant technically but if you are lacking in soft skills and no one wants to work with you then you are seriously limiting how far you can go. Soft skills are skills that enable you to work effectively and harmoniously with other people and they are incredibly important in accelerating your career in QA. Some specific examples of soft skills are:

- Problem-solving
- Communication
- Critical observation
- Leadership
- Collaboration
- Teamwork
- Empathy

Underlying these soft skills are what I call the three QA pillars of soft skills, these are:

- Communications, Succinctness
- Critical observation, Lack of bias
- Problem-solving, Customer focus

Like any skills, you need to work on them to improve, and the best way to learn is by doing. Get yourself out of your comfort zone; for example, with communication if you are not comfortable talking in front of a wide audience, start with smaller groups and just keep doing it.

Use the three pillars to underly your soft skills; for example, with your communications you want to get to the point, don't use 27 slides when 2 will get the message across.

Try to always have the bigger picture in mind; we may have 5 defects still in the system but will they stop us going live? What is the risk profile?

When communicating keep those questions in mind. In addition, you may have defect trend charts or performance output graphs in fabulous colours. What your stakeholders are looking for is your **interpretation** of these outputs, not the outputs themselves.

This is where your critical observation comes in. You may have different stakeholders, such as suppliers, claiming that the defects still remaining are a low risk, but it is on you to assert whether that is the case.

Impartiality and lack of bias in your reasoning, focusing entirely on the facts, will mean that not only do your stakeholders trust in what you say, they know that you are coming from a neutral position.

KEY TAKEAWAYS

√ Communications, get to the point!

√ Observe critically and independently.

√ Focus on what the customer needs (interpretation and expert guidance).

18 WRITING A GREAT BUG REPORT: TEST TECHNIQUES

One of my favourite interview questions is to ask the candidate what their 'best' bug was. By best, I mean what was the most impactful bug that you have caught in your career that if it had remained unnoticed and gone into live, all hell would have broken loose. However, my follow-on to that question was then 'How was this communicated and did it get the attention it needed?'

It's all very well finding a showstopper bug, but if your report is not coherent, to the point and definitive then it may not get the attention it needs. A great tester should always be able to create a great bug report. Don't assume I mean a three-page tome of what went wrong. A great bug report can be one paragraph.

To write a great bug report you need to bear some principles in mind

* **Keep it neutral in tone**. You are Switzerland, you don't lose your mind saying how terrible the issue is, the development team doesn't want your opinion, they want the facts. Keep it objective, not subjective.

* **Define the defect clearly**. Is it a performance defect, a UI defect a logical defect, calculation defect? Don't make the developer guess at what the initial problem is.

* **Are the steps taken to trigger the bug clear**? Have you left out a crucial step that means the bug may not appear in a reproducible manner?

* **Have you explained the dataset or datasets used to trigger the bug?** Can the bug be triggered regardless of data input or is it data specific?

* **Can you answer the following what, where, when and who questions in your bug report? (The Who could be user-role-related). The why is more complicated, see below.**

* **Don't lead the witness**. Where you have a strong suspicion as to the Why of a bug being triggered (for example, user permissions incorrectly defined), then do add this to the bug report; however, make it clear that you suspect it is due to this, no more.

* **Expected versus actual**. What did you expect to happen and what actually did happen. Too many bug reports state 'X, Y, Z happened', but then leave it there. Did we expect X, Y and Z to happen or did we only expect X and Y?

If you aren't confident in the clarity of your bug report, get it peer-reviewed. And preferably not by another tester but by a BA or developer. Ask them what is missing, how can the report be improved. When in doubt, clarify.

KEY TAKEAWAYS

✓ Cover the 4 Ws: what, where, when and who

✓ Expected versus actual, make sure this is included.

✓ If you believe you know the 5th W, namely Why, add it to report but make it clear that this is your assumption unless you know definitively that this is the root cause.

19 PROCESSES TO IMPROVE QA PROCESSES

> 'We are what we repeatedly do.
> Excellence then is not an act, but a habit.'
> – Aristotle

If you have a list of what you need to do and run through it every day then you are far less likely to get distracted and swayed by the events of the day. One excellent resource to look at is the **Checklist Manifesto** by Atul Gawande. He outlines the specifics of checklists and how you can use them to drive your day to be more productive.

With the focus and direction of QAT towards automation and DevOps, the need for clarity and structure remains key. Atul Gawande's thesis is that by breaking down complex tasks into simpler, easier to manage tasks in the form of a checklist, the quality bar is raised. Within QA this approach enables us to focus on being **effective and not efficient** (to quote Tim Ferriss), where we drill down on what we need to do and how we can make this happen. By transforming these tasks into a checklist, we work in a clearer, more focused way.

Aircraft in the 1940s and 1950s suffered major safety issues and the introduction of formalised, clear checklists for pilots dramatically improved safety. Gawande took this approach and used it within the surgical community to again raise the safety level in a remarkable way.

Applying this to QA is clear. Checklists for our strategic goals (for example, over one week) and checklists for our tactical goals. Examples could be:

Strategic

- Initial tool research for dataset automation (45)
- DevOps platform verification (post-build) (30)
- **Tactical**
- Review of projects statuses on Confluence (5)
- Project capacity planning for Project X and Y (15)
- Job description for automation engineer (10)

*The numbers indicate how long you should timebox each activity in minutes.

Strategic checklists are by their nature longer term and may take weeks or months to complete. Timeboxing them, for example, 45 minutes or 30 minutes, per day means that over a week you get traction and they are addressed in a structured manner. Or, you may work better allocating one block of time per week to do 'deep work' on these. It really is a matter of what works for you.

Tactical are usually repetitive tasks that you want to bake in so that they get done every day or the same time every week. These should be tasks that move the needle, always review them to make sure they are making you effective, not efficient.

KEY TAKEAWAYS

✓ Use checklists to maintain momentum.

✓ Timebox each item on your checklist.

✓ Don't worry about how you track your checklists: online, paper, whatever works for you.

20 JOINING IT UP AND LOOKING FOR THE BREAKS: INTEGRATION

One of the most exciting parts of large engineering work is joining the separate elements together, loading the propellant and doing a test fire. The US ballistic missile and then space programmes in the 1950s and 1960s had enormous issues with rockets exploding on the launch pads.

Every time there was an incident, a deep dive was held to find the root cause of the event. All of the individual components had been tested in isolation (unit and component tested) but the true test was incorporating these pieces into the final build.

For the Apollo program, there were over 5.5 million separate components, built by main contractors, such as Boeing, McDonnell Douglas and by thousands of subcontractors from around the world. The ultimate test in those days was to build them and fire it up and hope it didn't explode.

Just like massive engineering projects, in software development and QA, we don't have to wait until all pieces are integrated before we test them. We can exercise these elements through our unit tests, we can then link together subsets of them into component tests, then we can start integration tests. These integration tests can be discrete (one large area of the system, such as payments) or full integration (simulating customer order through to payment and fulfilment).

One of the key elements of integration testing is that there is an external dependency, for example, pulling data from a database, or connecting to another external system. The operative words here are **external dependencies**.

There are many tools that can be used for integration testing and they range from the very simple to the complex. To run integration tests, it is useful to know if the unit test has already been run and what framework they have been run against.

Katalon is one of the newer up and coming tools that provides effective test automaton/integration management. You can find it here: **https://www.katalon.com/** It is easy to deploy and supports most platforms (although cannot be used for desktop applications, the focus is more on Web and mobile).

If you are new to integration or automation, it makes sense to start small. Begin with a Jira Web application and build from there as it gives you the exposure to what is needed.

KEY TAKEAWAYS

✓ Exercise your external dependencies

✓ If you are Risk Based Testing look at prioritising integration testing.

✓ If your integration points aren't ready look at mocks/stubs to test them early on.

21 COMPANY CULTURE: OR AVOIDING REJECTION

> 'Company cultures are like country cultures.
> Never try to change one.
> Try, instead, to work with what you've got.'
> – Peter Drucker

Company culture is often nebulous, unwritten but pervasive in a group and organisation. It influences deeply how people interact, how they communicate and operate. How does this impact on you as a QA professional?

At its simplest it will influence how you share information, will describe escalation routes and what sort of control processes are used. I have worked in many different working cultures and one of the biggest stumbling blocks I have seen for new QAs entering a team or organisation is misreading the culture and, in turn, acting in ways that are non-aligned and, in turn, having very big difficulties in doing their best work.

One example I had was a QA engineer who was technically brilliant but dressed like he was going to the beach, turned up late and spoke in the abstract when the team needed specific action steps.

He was placed in a high-performing team that had a culture of tight control and while being agile and nominally agile were very clear in terms of their ways of working. It was rapidly clear that he simply did not fit the culture. The team rejected him very quickly and he had to move on.

However, the question was not that he should change himself totally to work well with the team. It was that he needed to adapt the ways in which he worked and communicated. Instead of talking in the abstract, he should have focused on how his great ideas could be made concrete. Instead of drafting lengthy papers on automation, he should have used the team whiteboard to explain after morning stand-up to the architects and developers his ideas.

So, one of the keys to getting a good feel for the culture of a team that you are joining as a QA professional is to ask some questions. Ideally, if you aren't the first QA to join the team, then spend time upfront with the existing QA professionals to get their views on expected ways of working and behaviours.

If you are the first QA to join the team, then there are specific cultural fit questions that you can ask:

KEY TAKEAWAYS

✓ How are communications handled? Read the room!

✓ Is everyone actively encouraged to take part in discussions?

✓ Do managers solicit and respond to input from everyone?

✓ Is management top-down or is it more consensus-driven?

22 MANAGEMENT: PROBLEM-SOLVING IN QA MANAGEMENT – THE THREE PS IN QA

When solving QA management problems, sometimes it is useful to have a mental model to work against in order to resolve problems that may occur. Within QA it can be useful to use the PPT triangle to determine if any of the three (or combinations of the three) are the cause of issues encountered.

This is a very simple construct. It looks at three areas which may be causing issues in project delivery, specifically:

- **People**
- **Processes**
- **Tools**

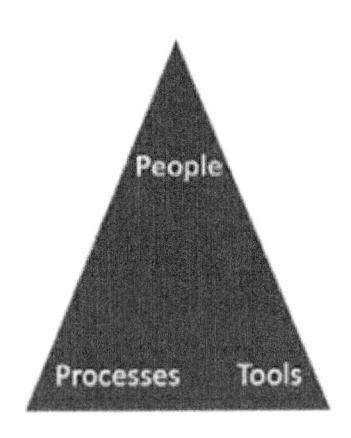

This is **not** to say that these are the only possible causes of issues; budgets, or lack thereof, for example, can be a major problem on QA projects. However, the PPT triangle is a handy shortcut when you are confronted with issues. Also, it is rare that there is one single root cause of issues, normally it is a combination of the above.

For example, QA projects persistently late in delivery from one team.

P P T

- Do you have the right people in terms of skills? Don't forget soft skills, they may be doing brilliantly technically but if they can't communicate well, you're toast.
- Are the right processes baked in? Are the team only having stand-ups once a week? Are issues following the right escalation routes?
- Are the right tools being used? Are we wedded to one specific tool when a combination would be better? Are we trying to automate everything even though there is a core of tests that would be better off doing manually?

Once you start digging, your next steps should become clearer.

KEY TAKEAWAYS

✓ Start with PPT.

✓ Be prepared for more than one root cause.

✓ Keep asking why until you get to the heart of the issue.

23 CONTINUOUS IMPROVEMENT (KAIZEN)

At its heart, every QAT project or programme we work on is trying to deliver something. It could be an app, it could be a system, it could be a hardware product. As we are executing testing or assuring testing, we should look at continuous improvement as a factor in how we raise the bar.

Continuous improvement, sometimes referred to as **kaizen** (from the Japanese for 'change for the good'), is the process by which we make small, incremental improvements to how we deliver, which, when added up make a massive difference. It's not big, it's not flashy but it really makes a difference. It drives us to become even better testers. If you improve by 1% a week, over time those small improvements really start to make a difference.

How can you do this? Retrospectives within agile are a great place to start if you are working in an agile environment. They are a ready source of areas for improvement. Pick one of the areas for improvement and look at how to incorporate this into the next sprint cycle. For waterfall implementations you can plan kaizen sessions at logical intervals, 2 weeks is usually a good rule of thumb.

To make this work you do have to formalise your kaizen process. Make a note of what you need to change, implement and then track it. This can be done in a spreadsheet, OneNote, Confluence dashboard, it doesn't really matter where you track it but it does matter how you track it.

Also, start small and don't worry if they appear overly simplistic. Remember, you are focussing on small changes that over time add up and make a massive (positive) difference. Also, make the process collaborative, imposed kaizen processes rarely work. That is why agile retrospectives are so valuable, you have the entire team there and key improvements are identified as a group.

A useful technique in running a kaizen event is first identifying the problem. Then, use the kaizen tree of analysis, specifically using the **what, where, who, how** and **when** approach.

The problem: 'Too many defects being found in the UAT cycle, we should be catching these earlier.'

What are we using to find these defects?

Where are the defects being found? Are they clustered in a specific area?

Who do the defects impact? One specific group or all users?

How are they being found? Can we use a form of these test cases in earlier test phases? For example, at the system or integration layers?

When are they being found? What is unique about the UAT phase that we aren't capturing earlier on in our tests?

KEY TAKEAWAYS

√ Use the kaizen analysis tree to help guide your kaizen analysis.

√ Formalise and record your findings.

√ Do it on a scheduled basis.

√ Make sure results are distributed across your team(s).

24 RISK MITIGATION: STOP IT GOING WRONG BEFORE IT DOES

Risk mitigation is a key element of any testing project. It focuses minds on what can go wrong and why. Within QA we are focused on what doesn't work and why. However, before we start a QA project, a clear focus on risk mitigation helps you and the team, regardless of size, to focus on what could go wrong and how to minimize the impact on delivery. Note that this is not about risk-based testing, that is covered in Section 4. This covers QA delivery risk and how to mitigate this risk.

For example, the system under test is large and complex. We have a team of five QA people, a mix of functional and automation engineers. One of the QA team, Mary, is the most senior automation engineer. She has worked on numerous previous releases and is viewed as the most expert person within the team.

However, Mary is a contractor and has hinted in the past that she may move soon to another contract. This is a risk we need to look at mitigating. In this case, closer shadowing of Mary by other members of the automation team and focusing on the gaps in their knowledge would help. This can be done diplomatically, always with the view that eliminating single person risk in any project is key.

The advantage of thinking about risks upfront is that if they do turn into issues, it is far more likely that measures to mitigate them have already been thought about. However, the ideal process is to prevent risks turning into issues at all. Good practice is to analyse what you believe will be your top 5 risks.

Use **PPT** to help guide you in this approach, **people**, **processes** and **technology**. For example,

- **People**: we won't have QA team fully staffed by time project starts.
- **Processes**: the PM is insisting on a form of wagile (waterfall/agile)
- **Technology:** there's no budget for one of our key accessibility tools.

One additional approach for risk mitigation is to look at pre- and post-risk mitigation:

For example: risk of Mary leaving.

Pre-risk mitigation: more knowledge sharing and paired programming.

Post-risk mitigation: close relationship with contractor supplier agency, pre-vetting of possible candidates.

KEY TAKEAWAYS

✓ Bug bash timeboxed in sprint plan.

✓ Look at root causes, any clustering?

✓ Kaizen, what can you learn from this sprint that can improve quality the next sprint?

25 DEFECTS ADDING TO THE PRODUCT BACKLOG AND THE RISK TO YOUR PROJECT

A common issue in software projects is where you have defects adding to the overall product backlog backlogs. The QA team continue to raise defects but the sheer volume of defects means the project's leads push them to the back of the queue and they don't get addressed within sprints in a timely manner.

The overall lead responsible for backlog grooming – that is, what is in or out in the upcoming sprint – will always have a tension between building new functionality (that is always cool and popular) and fixing existing defects (definitely not cool or in any way popular).

Bear in mind that the product backlog 'lists all features, functions, requirements, enhancements, and fixes that constitute the changes to be made to the product' (from www.scrumguides.org). That's a pretty broad spectrum of elements a product manager needs to consider. What are the risks then if your defect count keeps climbing and you aren't getting defects addressed in a timely manner?

- The project is not giving an accurate representation of its delivery status. It may be reporting 75% complete but a large defect backlog makes this almost impossible to stick to.
- The high rate of defects may require a fundamental reworking of the system being developed, in itself increasing the risk of system regression.

- There is likely to be defect clustering, a phenomenon whereby defects cluster in a specific area. You can find out quite easily if this is the case through reviewing your defect management tool and filtering on description or functional area. You will very likely see a spike (Pareto style) of root causes.
- There is always the risk that defects are larger than you thought they were originally after you spend more time examining them.
- As a result, you need to consider possible solutions, such as:
- Negotiate with project leads to set aside a specific time per week to work on defects. The dev team will likely be familiar with this as a 'bug bash' session.
- Deep dive on root cause for your defect clustering: is there a specific functional area causing the majority of issues and could this be resolved through increasing your unit testing code coverage or paired programming techniques?
- Once you get on top of defect count, look at what changes you think should be made in processes to prevent a reoccurrence of the issues you encountered.

KEY TAKEAWAYS

√ Bug bash timeboxed in sprint plan

√ Look at root causes, any clustering?

√ Kaizen, what can you learn from this sprint that can improve quality the next sprint?

26 KEEPING IT ALL ON TRACK: DAILY, WEEKLY AND MONTHLY TASKS

There are specific tasks you can do to keep your test project or programme management on track. If you make these part of your routines on a daily, weekly and monthly basis it then frees you up to respond rapidly and dynamically to issues as they arise.

You can and should flex the tasks as your project or programme requires but having a starting structure gives you flexibility in this approach. Use the following to help guide your processes.

Some examples of daily tasks:

Task #	Description	Schedule
1	**Morning stand-up**: blockers and plans for the day	10 mins
2	**Finance tracker verification**	10 mins
3	**Resource allocation review**	10 mins

Weekly tasks:

Task #	Description	Schedule
1	**Documentation review/assurance. 3 times per week.**	30 to 60 mins
2	**Deep dive:** one selected project: Review with QAT manager the tactical plans for their project. This should cover resourcing, planning, financing and overall QAT strategy. Outputs should be clearly defined actions.	30 to 60 mins
3	**QAT lunch and learn:** invite all members of co-located QAT teams to a recurring weekly lunch and learn. Keep the agenda very open (for example, 'AI and testing') and informal. The idea is to foment free-flowing conversations and cross-fertilisation of ideas.	30 to 60 mins
4	**Customer checkpoint** meeting. Touchpoint with customer to address risks, issues and observations. Depending on customer needs, the frequency of this may be lessened; however,	30 to 60 mins

		as a first step this should be a weekly activity.	
5		**Feedback session** for selected member of team. Follow 80/20 rule, they should speak for 80% of the team. Use open-ended questions, such as '**What do you think we should do to improve the efficacy of Project X from a QAT perspective?**' Set SMART objectives and schedule next meeting at this meeting. *Note, for large teams, over 30 members, delegate these sessions to senior QAT leaders while you as programme manager conduct them for these leaders.	20 to 30 mins

Monthly tasks:

Task #	Description	Schedule
1	**QAT senior leadership team meeting**: attendees should be all QAT delivery owners. Aim is to focus on strategic initiatives, do not get bogged down into day-to-day operational issues, these should be managed outside of this forum. Strategic initiatives should focus on themes such as: • QAT automation tooling implementation • Data management and privacy • Skills gaps and knowledge sharing. Outputs and actions **must** be tracked. Allocate a KRI (key responsible individual) to each action and follow up at next meeting.	2 to 3 hrs
2	**Deep dive** on all finance projections and review against existing projections. Examine historic projects	2 to 3 hrs

	and review where there have been variances and look to understand why. Outputs of this should inform future finance planning with the aim of making this more accurate.	
3	**Deep dive** on automation tooling.	2 to 3 hrs
4	**Deep dive** on customer project/programme projections.	2 to 3 hrs

27 TRACKING QA PROJECT PROGRESS (WATERFALL)

As your QA project progresses there are elements that need to be monitored.

- Schedule/delivery (to plan)
- Costs (to budget)
- Defect rate (expected versus actual)

If we chart these together, we can get a clearer view on how our QA project is performing. We should chart each on a scale of 1 to 4.

A project schedule on track would be a 2, the perfect score. Over schedule would be 3, very late is 4.

Ahead of schedule is 1. Colour coding is recommended as it keeps clarity on progress.

So, for example, if Project A is on schedule it would be a 2.

```
1       2           3           4
```

Schedule

For costs (to budget) we are over budget so we mark it as a 3.

```
1       2           3           4
```

Costs

For defects this one is trickier. We expect an inverted bell curve for defect counts, the earlier in the project, the more defects we should be finding. This is not an exact science and there is an element of subjectivity to this one. You should look at the trends in your defects, are they increasing, decreasing or steady state?

Compare this to the test phase that you are in and use your judgement.

For this sample project we are looking at we are in the system test phase and our defect rate is decreasing week on week. So, we will give this a 2.

Defects

1   2   3   4

If we then add together our scores, 2 for schedule, 3 for costs and 2 for defects, we have a total of 7. This will then give us our baseline (assuming we are starting the project) and will give us a weekly barometer of project health.

1   6   12

Overall Project View

If you set this as a weekly practice, your view of what is occurring within your project is enhanced.

KEY TAKEAWAYS

✓ Remember the lower the number the better.

✓ Use colours.

✓ Look at trends with defects over the week, spikes and toughs then are smoothed.

28 STAND-UPS: THE POWER OF INTROVERTS

'Not all who are silent do not want to talk.'

– Debasish Mridha

Stand-ups are critical to the smooth running of agile delivery. Run well and they are a great way of making sure everyone is clear on the tactical plans for the day ahead. Run badly and they are anything but agile (or agile) and dissolve into endless technical discussions and leave everyone confused.

A stand-up, distilled to its essence, is a way of focusing on two things:

1. Plans for the day

2. Any blockers happening now (or likely to happen today.)

That's it.

They aren't designed for Joe and Samantha to dive into very specific detail about how the upcoming change to the GUI will work and the impact on users. Or for Bob and Sarah to discuss the details of their firewall router changes and the order in which these changes should be made.

Some rules for running effective stand-ups;

- Everyone has the chance to speak: make sure that your more reticent, less vocal members of the team are given this chance. They may be the least vocal but often have the most relevant information.
- Keep it short, 10 to 15 minutes should be the maximum time allocated.
- Have one person running the stand-up, you can't do this by committee.
- Stand-up! I've been amazed at how many stand-ups I've attended in the past where people have sat down. This doesn't work, the sense of urgency dictated by everyone standing up is lost. Take the chairs away, don't give people the opportunity to sit down.
- Keep your remote people involved. Have them dial in via Skype or other messaging system. Just because they aren't there in person doesn't mean you leave them out of the loop.
- Keep people on track, you only want to know 2 things, plans for the day and blockers.
- Don't let unblocking blockers raised blow your 10 to 15 minute timeslot. If three out of your ten people can solve the major blocker get them to meet right after the stand-up. Don't waste the other seven's time.
- Keep it tight, keep people focused on the day ahead.

KEY TAKEAWAYS

✓ Stick to the process, plans and blockers, and time allocated.

✓ Stay on time.

✓ Breakout sessions with smaller group to discuss details of blockers.

29 EFFECTIVE COMMUNICATION

They can be the bane of our lives, but as it stands, emails are still a key part of communications within QA. Start using Slack or other online messaging systems as well and there is a real risk of overload.

Within QA, knowing how everything is tracking has traditionally been done via email. This has its advantages; however, with the volume of emails that need to be tracked, it is easy for key information to be lost. It's good to look at alternatives to email, for example:

Collaboration software: team updates can be made in Confluence or Trello (Trello is very task-based so more focus on what needs to be done, for example, within an agile backlog, rather than updates).

Confluence is particularly useful for sharing best practice, templates and project updates as well as for others to pose questions they need help with. For example, recommendations for compatibility tools that others in the team may have used.

Using Slack as a communications tool suffers from the same issue as email, constant checking of it can distract you from core 'deep' work. The default settings in Slack mean that you can be constantly bombarded with messages. Instead, turn off mobile notifications and get very used to the 'Pause notifications' option.

Walk and talk: if co-located it can be easier to talk instead of email. Amazing how many teams still send emails when talking to the person very near them achieves the same aim.

Morning stand-ups: hold a daily stand-up if you have one team. If you have multiple teams then make sure each has its own stand-up.

Weekly catch up: slightly longer session that enables everyone to ask questions in relation to strategy but also to look at solving problems. When you have a larger group of QA experts this becomes your pool for everyone to ask about tools others may have used, approaches to problems that others may have encountered and generally share knowledge.

If you **have** to email, some tips:

Rule of 5 sentences: no email should have more than 5 sentences in it. This forces everyone to be more concise. If they have a report or more lengthy document then attach it and send as such. But if it is project information then go with 5. This forces a degree of discipline and removes waffle.

Rule of 3: check your email 3 times a day. This is Tim Ferriss's idea of reducing interruptions and letting you focus on deep work. Check at 10 a.m., 1 p.m. and 4 p.m. (assuming a standard working day). Make it clear to your team that if they need an urgent response, they should call you.

KEY TAKEAWAYS

✓ Explore alternatives to email for effective communication.

✓ Schedule regular catchups.

✓ Think of the Rule of 5 and the Rule of 3 when emailing.

30 FINANCE: BUDGETS AND QA

Not many QA staff get excited about managing and planning budgets for their projects, but, like flossing or eating veggies, you gotta do it. The usual differences between agile and waterfall apply; however, whatever form of delivery, you will need to keep within the boundaries of your budget.

Resources will likely be the single biggest aspect of your budget, unless you are also planning on going crazy and buying that hot new AI tool that everyone is raving about!

Tools don't need to get more complicated than Excel for creating and maintaining budgets. However, if you are looking at sharing and maintaining your budgets across your teams there are some great plug-ins for Confluence, such as:

https://marketplace.atlassian.com/apps/216/excel-for-confluence, which really help visualisation of where you are going and keep your team up to date on budgets.

Like pretty much every aspect of QA, getting involved early makes a big difference. You need ways to measure, report and track QA budgets within your team or across multiple teams. Some of the most effective ways I have done this and seen it done have been weekly planned versus actual budgetary reviews. By planning these on a weekly basis, the potential for costs to run ahead of planned are limited.

When setting a budget, you have some options; however, these only apply where you have previous data to work from. Where you have this data, your accuracy should be high as you can see the variance in budgeted versus actual.

1) Based on last year's numbers. In other words, how accurate (or inaccurate) were you?

2) Based on last year's numbers plus x%. We had 3 teams last year, we are starting up another team so it is a straight 25% increase, or is your headcount much higher in the fourth team?

3) A percentage of your overall IT budget. Numbers I have used in the past have ranged from 20% to 25%. When pushed back on this, a useful trick is to ask what the cost to the company of releasing buggy software will be.

4) A percentage of the development team size. This will be strongly influenced by whether your delivery team is agile or waterfall (usually your ratio of testers to developers will be higher in an agile team).

Some common mistakes you should look to avoid in budgeting:

- **Forgetting about overtime costs**. Especially towards the end of a final release, there is huge pressure to complete testing, factor this into your planning.
- **Cost increases**. If you are running a long project (+1 year), does your budget cover any uplift in resourcing, licensing or other costs that need to be factored in?
- **Assumptions**. Are you baking in any assumptions into your budgetary forecast? If so, make that explicit to the person who needs to approve the budget.

KEY TAKEAWAYS

✓ Get involved early and use Excel.

✓ If you have historic budgetary data use it.

✓ Watch your assumptions.

31 PRODUCTIVITY: THE POWER OF NEXT ACTION STEPS – KEEPING MOMENTUM

One constant problem with QA management is the demand on your times and maintaining productivity throughout the day. There are constant interruptions to your time and the need to stay on track is key, otherwise, you will not achieve what you need to in order to deliver your QA project.

Staying on track can be helped by having very specific, next action steps for your project. I like to work with lists of less than 5, very specific action steps. These are ideally steps that take no longer than twenty minutes to complete.

The idea is that after dealing with the standard interruptions that occur during a day, you can pick the next action off the list without losing momentum in your next steps. This is incredibly valuable in getting what you need to do in order to get your project moving and on track. An awful lot of time is taken to reset your mind when you are interrupted. Having a defined set of next action steps allows you to reset quickly and efficiently.

An example of a next action step list would be the following:

- Draft QA plan for peer review
- Defect review prep for call with product owner and lead developer
- Resource profile review and plans for next 3 months

- Budget review for this month (planned versus actual) as month almost over
- Review costings for new browser compatibility tool

In addition, as you have these actions time blocked (i.e. when your allotted time on the action is completed you move on to the next item), you are more likely to complete each action. Work expands to fill the time allotted to it, if you have tight control over this then you are more likely to complete each one in turn. Once you have worked through your list then take five minutes to create your next 5 action step lists so you make it very much rinse and repeat.

Even if some of your next action steps carry over into the next day or days, that is not an issue. For example, the first on my list above, 'Draft QA plan for peer review', will in itself have a number of steps. So, once you have drafted the plan, mark that as done on your list.

The next step, 'Circulate for peer review', should then go to the bottom of the list. Thus, as you work through your items you have only 5 items on your action list at any one time. Don't agonise over the priority of these actions, rather focus on each in turn. You may of course replace with an urgent action one of your existing actions, it isn't meant to restrict you, rather to act as a sea chart for you to guide your ship to the next spot on the map.

The aim is to maintain momentum and not lose focus on what needs to get done as opposed to what actually gets done. This is part of the difference between being busy and being productive.

KEY TAKEAWAYS

✓ Only have 5 next action steps.

✓ Work through in turn, don't worry about priority.

✓ Maintain the list in an easy to access tool such as OneNote.

32 MANAGEMENT: DELEGATION

A key aspect of QA management is working with your team to set goals. The idea is that for any QAT project it should be straightforward to set out what the goals of the QA professional are and to make sure that they are aligned to the project. This list of goals should be succinct and clear. The aims of this are twofold:

1) Delegated responsibility with accountability and clarity.

2) Your team are very clear on what the tactical and strategic aims of the project are.

Too often I have seen in QA projects where managers have delegated responsibility yet have not outlined what they define as success. So, they are saying, '**Look, you're in charge, but I have no idea how we will know if everything has gone to plan or not**'. They haven't formed the expectation boundaries and so, inevitably, they step in when their QA person is not doing what they expect them to do.

Don't be that manager. Spend some time with your QA professional, set out your thoughts in terms of tactical and strategic success and jointly work up a list of what you think are the top five goals for the project or programme. Each goal should be no longer than a few sentences.

Each of these ideally will not only focus on that person's strengths but will also have some stretch elements to them; for example, if they haven't conducted accessibility testing before, have that as a stretch goal for them to achieve.

This is really simple yet also very effective. You are empowering your people and giving them clear information on what success looks like. What you aren't doing is micromanaging them and telling them how to deliver their project, you are relying on their skills and experience to do this.

However, to make this work you also need to have a follow-up session, two weeks is a good time period. This gives them time to make progress but also enables them to check in with you for potential refining of goals and collaborative analysis of progress.

When you have a process for iterative planning and then follow-up review, you will then have a clear way in which you are delegating but not leaving people exposed and unsure of what they need to do. This moves away from being busy to being productive.

KEY TAKEAWAYS

- ✓ Set clear expectation boundaries.
- ✓ Confirm the individual being managed understands these and always has the opportunity to clarify what these are.
- ✓ Include stretch goals.
- ✓ Review every two weeks with them.

33 MANAGEMENT: THE FEEDBACK LOOP 3 TO 1 RULE

> 'In a growth mindset, challenges are exciting rather than threatening. So rather than thinking, oh, I'm going to reveal my weaknesses, you say, wow, here's a chance to grow.'
>
> – Carol Dweck

This is actually a combination of multiple concepts in management and directly applicable to QA management as a way of running a team, regardless of size.

The rule is effectively the ratio in which you provide feedback and inform on how you want things to improve. Very often, once we have teams up and running, we wait for someone to do something wrong, we reprimand them and move on. This is not massively motivating as you are intervening only at a **negative** level.

Instead of this approach, a far more effective method is to catch people doing things right. You call out the positive actions, outcomes or behaviours either to that person individually, or even better to that person in front of their team. This positive reinforcement inevitably increases motivation levels as you are intervening with a positive message, in other words coaching. It's remarkable how calling out even the smallest things, such as running an effective defect board session, acts as a motivator.

As a result, for every one time where you need to step in negatively (course correction), you should be looking at calling out good actions at least three times as much.

A valid question within the QA space is how can we do this if we have an underperforming team? Won't it be very difficult as inevitably you will be focused on managing the problems within the team and looking at how these issues can be resolved?

The answer is to start small. If you have a team with clear issues you will be giving feedback about how they can improve performance. However, even in a team like this, there will be behaviours and actions that you should be able to call out positively. Even as small as running effective planning sessions, good customer interactions or professionalism in requirements clarification. The key is nothing is too small that it does not warrant praise.

If you consistently focus on the negative aspects of what is being done, or not done, this quite naturally has a negative impact on team and individual morale. While you will have to call out and set specific areas for improvement, the minute you start seeing progress and improvements you should start calling these out loud and clear

KEY TAKEAWAYS

- ✓ Don't always focus on the negative elements when looking to improve QA team or individual performance.
- ✓ Look to balance 1 element of criticism with 3 parts praise when giving individual or team feedback.
- ✓ Start small, build on and call out good behaviours whenever possible.
- ✓ Look to transition to a coaching mindset, where you reinforce what you wish to see happen and calling out people's strengths.

APPENDIX A

- Getting Things Done: The Art of Stress-Free Productivity by David Allen
- The New One-Minute Manager by Kenneth Blanchard and Spencer Johnson
- The 4-Hour Workweek by Timothy Ferriss
- Specification by Example by Gojko Adzic
- Test Estimation:
    - Softwaretestinghelp.com
    - Tryqa.com
    - Softwaretestpro.com

Printed in Great Britain
by Amazon